ScottFore
Literacy

SANDRA J. BRIGGS
San Mateo Union High School District
San Mateo, California

MAYRA L. MENÉNDEZ, ED.S
The School Board of Broward County
Florida

ScottForesman
A Division of HarperCollinsPublishers

I would like to thank Chicoche Huipio and all of the other ESL students who have made the teaching of English and literacy an adventure and a joy. This book is dedicated to Eileen Peters, Mary Jane Maples, and Gloria Johnson, whose friendship and dedication to quality educational materials have been a constant inspiration to me.

Sandra J. Briggs

I would like to thank my parents, Emma and Ramón, for their gift of an education in this country. A special thank you to my sister, Neida, for her encouragement in all my endeavors and to my nephews and nieces, Richard, Robert, Julie, and Stephanie, for being a part of my life. Thanks to my friends and colleagues for sharing their knowledge and to the staff at ScottForesman for their support and commitment to this project.

Mayra L. Menéndez

CONSULTING REVIEWERS

Andrés A. Alonso, *Samuel L. Berliner School*
Newark, New Jersey

Marilyn Bach, *New York City Public Schools*
New York City, New York

Denise Graham, *Austin Independent School District*
Austin, Texas

Deborah J. Hasson, *Florida International University*
Miami, Florida

Nancy Kodama, *Los Angeles Unified School District*
Los Angeles, California

Virginia Rodríguez, *Fort Worth Independent School District*
Fort Worth, Texas

Stephen H. Shiu, Ph.D., *Chicago Board of Education*
Chicago, Illinois

ILLUSTRATIONS

21–28: Mike Edsey; **29–36:** Dennis Franzen; **5–12, 61–68:** Mitch Heinze; **13–20, 53–60:** Tom McKee; **1, 5, 21, 29, 37–44, 45, 53, 61, 69:** Christian Musselman; **37–44:** Jim Wisneiwski; **45–52, 69–76:** John Zielinski.

PHOTOGRAPHS

5TR: © Larry Kolvoord/The Image Works; **5BL, 5BR, 6, 10, 13TL, 13BR, 14T:** © Elizabeth Crews; **13BL, 13BC:** David W. Hamilton/The Image Bank; **14BR:** Sobel/Klonsky/The Image Bank; **21:** Bob Daemmrich/Tony Stone Images; **22B:** Henley & Savage/Tony Stone Images; **34:** Steve Leonard/Tony Stone Images; **69:** Bob Daemmrich/The Image Works *(salesperson)*; **69:** Margot Granitsas/The Image Works *(checkout person)*; **69, 75:** Larry Dale Gordon/ The Image Bank *(receptionist)*; **69, 71:** Stuart Cohen/Comstock *(child-care worker)*; **69, 71:** Bob Daemmrich/Tony Stone Images *(restaurant worker)*, /The Image Works *(data-entry clerk)*; **69, 71:** Richard Hutchings/Photo Researchers *(waitress)*; **69, 71:** Lee F. Snyder/Photo Researchers *(delivery truck driver)*; **74, 75:** Jeff Greenberg/Photo Researchers *(medical technician, mechanic)*; **74, 75:** Jeffrey Coolidge/The Image Bank *(bank teller)*; **74, 75:** Lawrence Migdale/Photo Researchers *(high school computer class)*.

CONTENTS

Getting Started 1
- To understand *same* and *different*
- To recognize numbers
- To recognize letters of the alphabet

UNIT 1 **School** 5
- To identify school facilities and personnel
- To recognize words related to school
- To ask where a room is located
- To write one's name

UNIT 2 **Class Schedules** 13
- To identify classes
- To tell time
- To identify days of the week
- To recognize words in a class schedule and a student form
- To talk about class schedules
- To write one's address

UNIT 3 **Emergencies** 21
- To identify types of emergencies
- To recognize words related to emergencies
- To make an emergency phone call
- To give personal information
- To write phone numbers

UNIT 4 **Health** 29
- To understand medical information
- To identify the months of the year
- To recognize words related to doctors and dentists
- To ask a health professional for information
- To write one's date of birth

UNIT 5 **Family** 37
- To identify members of a family
- To recognize words for family members
- To recognize words for stages of development (baby to adult)
- To talk about one's family
- To write names of people in one's family

UNIT 6 **Food** 45
- To identify kinds of food
- To order from a fast-food restaurant menu
- To recognize food words
- To identify amounts of money
- To talk about how much food costs
- To write the word for one's favorite food

UNIT 7 **Shopping** 53
- To identify types of stores
- To identify items one can buy
- To ask for information about shopping
- To read prices on price tags and sales slips
- To know how to use checks and credit cards
- To write a short shopping list

UNIT 8 **Getting Things Done** 61
- To know how to get a driver's license
- To recognize words on traffic signs
- To know how to get a library card
- To understand post office procedures
- To say what one needs at a library or post office
- To address an envelope

UNIT 9 **Jobs** 69
- To identify types of jobs
- To recognize words related to jobs
- To know how to look for a job
- To know how to find training for a job
- To ask for information about jobs
- To write words for jobs in which one is interested

Same and Different

These shoes are the same.

These shoes are different.

 Circle the shoe that is different.

 Circle the shoe that is the same.

Numbers

1　2　3　4　5　6　7　8　9　10　11　12

 Circle the number that is the same.

1	4	9	(1)	7		**7**	4	9	1	7
2	8	2	7	1		**8**	8	2	9	1
3	8	5	9	3		**9**	6	5	9	3
4	4	7	1	2		**10**	11	7	10	1
5	2	5	8	6		**11**	12	11	1	10
6	8	9	2	6		**12**	11	1	2	12

 Count and circle. Trace the number.

2

5

10

3

9

The Alphabet: Capital Letters

A B C D E F G H I J K L M N
O P Q R S T U V W X Y Z

 Circle the letter that is the same.

B	P	(B)	E	R	**H**	M	H	K	X
W	A	M	W	V	**C**	C	O	D	G
T	E	T	Z	J	**S**	Z	R	Y	S
Q	Q	C	G	R	**L**	F	L	E	T
R	P	E	R	B	**N**	W	K	N	M

The Alphabet: Small Letters

a b c d e f g h i j k l m n
o p q r s t u v w x y z

 Circle the letter that is the same.

a	o	c	e	(a)	**j**	g	p	j	i
p	q	p	g	y	**e**	c	o	u	e
l	i	t	f	l	**d**	h	d	b	q
k	h	k	b	d	**u**	n	v	u	x
m	w	n	r	m	**g**	g	q	y	p
f	f	t	l	k	**o**	e	a	o	c

The Alphabet: Capital Letters and Small Letters

A a B b C c D d E e F f G g H h I i J j
K k L l M m N n O o P p Q q R r S s
T t U u V v W w X x Y y Z z

 Circle the small letter.

A	c	u	(a)	o	**N**	m	n	u	w
B	d	b	p	q	**O**	e	c	p	o
C	e	o	a	c	**P**	d	q	p	d
D	b	d	q	p	**Q**	b	d	o	q
E	e	c	o	a	**R**	r	i	l	j
F	l	i	f	k	**S**	e	k	s	c
G	g	y	j	q	**T**	l	t	f	i
H	b	h	k	d	**U**	m	v	u	n
I	f	t	l	i	**V**	v	w	x	u
J	j	l	i	t	**W**	u	v	w	y
K	b	h	k	d	**X**	w	n	y	x
L	i	l	t	f	**Y**	v	y	k	z
M	n	v	u	m	**Z**	w	v	z	y

school

classroom

hall

office

 Listen to the teacher. Do the actions.

Point to the school.
Point to the hall.
Point to the office.

 Trace the word. Name the letters.

school

hall

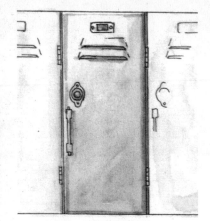

locker

custodian

rest room

rest room

 Say the conversation.

A: Excuse me. Where's the rest room?

B: It's down this hall.

A: Thank you.

 Trace the word. Name the letters.

custodian

Draw a line.

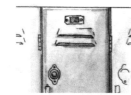　　　LOCKER　　　　　　　　　　rest room

1. 　　REST ROOM　　　　　　　custodian

2. 　　CUSTODIAN　　　　　　　locker

3. 　　GIRLS　　　　　　　　　boys

4. 　　BOYS　　　　　　　　　girls

 Circle the word.

　　　　hall
　　　（school）

1. 　custodian

　　　hall

2. 　locker

　　　rest room

3. 　boys

　　　girls

4. 　custodian

　　　boys

classroom   teacher   student

board   pencil   pen   students   book

Listen to the teacher. Do the actions.

Close your books.
Open your books to page 8.
Take out a pencil.

Trace the word. Name the letters.

book

Circle the word.

 **1.**   classroom

rest room

2.    pencil

book

 **3.**   teacher

student

4.   locker

pencil

 **5.**   pen

board

 Draw a line.

 1.

board

 2.

students

 3.

book

 **4.**

pen

5.

teacher

office

principal

secretary

desk

form

Name _Ana López_

name

 Say the conversation.

A: What's your name?
B: Ana López.
A: Hi, Ana. Please write your name here.
B: OK.

 Trace the word. Name the letters.

form

Circle the word.

 1.   office
         hall

2.   student
         principal

 3.   name
         desk

4.    teacher
         secretary

 5.   form
         office

 Draw a line.

 1.   form

2. **Name** *Ana López*   secretary

 3.   desk

 4.   principal

 5.   name

Write the letter. Say the word.

1.  __ e s k

2. __ u s t o d i a n

3.  __ o a r d

4. __ i r l

5.  __ e c r e t a r y

6.  __ o r m

 Write your name.

_____

  Ask 2 classmates to write their names.

1._____

2._____

Unit 2: Class Schedules

English

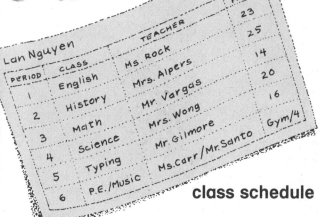

Lan Nguyen			ROOM
PERIOD	CLASS	TEACHER	
1	English	Ms. Rock	23
2	History	Mrs. Alpers	25
3	Math	Mr. Vargas	14
4	Science	Mrs. Wong	20
5	Typing	Mr. Gilmore	16
6	P.E./Music	Ms. Carr/Mr. Santo	Gym/4

class schedule

history

math

science

Listen to the teacher. Do the actions.

Stand up.
Sit down.
Raise your hand.

Trace the word. Name the letters.

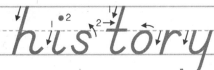

P.E.

typing

music

Sunday	Monday	Tuesday	Wednesday	Thursday	Friday	Saturday
	P.E.	Music	P.E.	Music	P.E.	

days of the week

 Say the conversation.

A: When do you have music class?
B: Period 6 on Tuesday and Thursday.
A: Where is the music class?
B: It's in Room 4.

 Trace the word. Name the letters.

room

▲▲

Listen to the teacher. Circle the day of the week.

Sunday	Friday	Tuesday	Wednesday	Monday	Friday	Wednesday
Tuesday	Monday	Thursday	Friday	Thursday	Tuesday	Saturday

Draw a line.

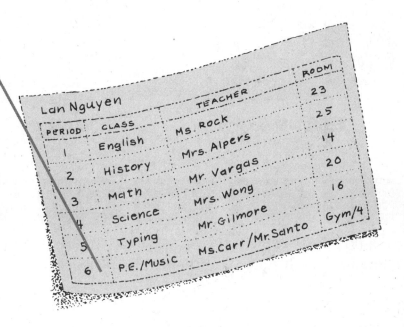

Lan Nguyen

PERIOD	CLASS	TEACHER	ROOM
1	English	Ms. Rock	23
2	History	Mrs. Alpers	25
3	Math	Mr. Vargas	14
4	Science	Mrs. Wong	20
5	Typing	Mr. Gilmore	16
6	P.E./Music	Ms.Carr/Mr.Santo	Gym/4

clock

watch

hour   **minutes**

8:00 A.M.

8:00 P.M.

I have English at 8:00.

8:00
English

9:05
history

9:55
math

10:50
science

11:45
lunch

1:00
typing

1:45
P.E.

 Say the conversation.

A: What time is it?
B: It's almost eight o'clock.
A: It's time for English class.
B: Let's go.

What time is it?

 Trace the word. Name the letters.

Draw a line.

1.   `3:30`

2.   `7:55`

3.   `10:15`

4.   `2:25`

5.   `11:40`

 Listen to the teacher. Circle the clock.

1.  `4:10`    `3:40`    `3:20`

2.  `8:15`    `7:45`    `8:45`

3. `11:05`   `11:25`   `10:55`

4. `5:35`   `6:35`   `6:25`

5. `4:50`   `5:10`   `4:10`

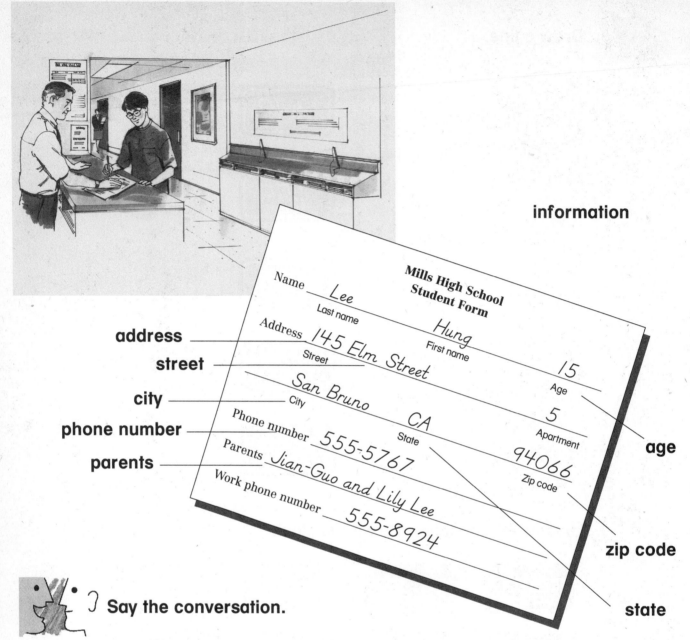

information

Mills High School
Student Form

Name _____ Lee _____
Last name

Address ___ 145 Elm Street
Street

City ___ San Bruno ___

Phone number ___ 555-5767

Parents ___ Jian-Guo and Lily Lee

Work phone number ___ 555-8924

Hung
First name

15
Age

CA
State

5
Apartment

94066
Zip code

address
street
city
phone number
parents

age
zip code
state

 Say the conversation.

A: Hello. What's your name?

B: Hung Lee.

A: OK, Hung. Here's your class schedule. Please fill in the information requested on this form.

Trace the word. Name the letters.

parents

 **Draw a line.**

16

Sánchez

San Mateo

439 Ash Street

Juan and
Cilia Sánchez

**Mills High School
Student Form**

Name _____

        Last name   First name   Age

Address _____

        Street   Apartment

_____

        City   State   Zip code

Phone number _____

Parents _____

Work phone number _____

María

Work:
  555-5876

94402

555-0129

California

 Circle the word.

1. Jian-Guo and Lily Lee   parents   name

2. 145 Elm Street   street   city

3. 555-5767   zip code   phone number

4. Lee, Hung   city   name

5. 15   age   zip code

Write the letter. Say the word.

1. ___ i s t o r y

2.  ___ i p   c o d e

3.  ___ a t c h

4.  ___ o o m

5.  ___ e n c i l

6. ___ y p i n g

 Write your street address.

_____

- -

_____

 Ask 2 classmates to write their street addresses.

1. _____

2. _____

Unit 3: Emergencies

accident

drowning

fire

Call 911 in an emergency.

burn

 Listen to the teacher. Do the actions.

Touch your arm.
Touch your leg.
Touch your head.

 Trace the word. Name the letters.

emergency

medical emergency

phone book

poison

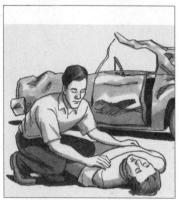

traffic accident

Call 0 for the operator.

natural disaster

 Say the conversation.

A: Operator, my mother is very sick.
B: Where are you?
A: Our address is 367 Oak Street, Apartment 10.
B: Please stay on the phone.

 Trace the word. Name the letters.

phone book

Draw a line.

1.    drowning

2.    poison

3.    traffic accident

4.    fire

 Circle the word.

1.    operator   phone book

2.    natural disaster   accident

3.    operator   poison

4.    drowning   accident

HELP!

victim

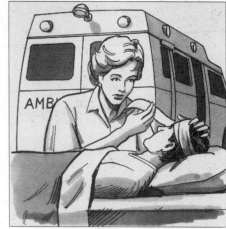
paramedic   first aid

rescue   firefighter

police officer

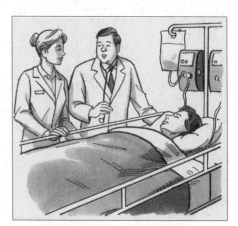
nurse   doctor

Listen to the teacher. Do the actions.

Point to the victim.
Point to the police officer.
Point to the paramedic.

Trace the word. Name the letters.

nurse

Draw a line.

1.    paramedic

2.    doctor

3.    firefighter

4. 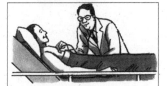   police officer

 Circle the word.

1.    paramedic   victim

2.    doctor   police officer

3.    firefighter   police officer

4.    nurse   paramedic

Where can I get help?

Red Cross

hospital

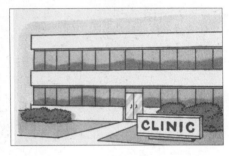

clinic

ambulance

fire station

police station

 Say the conversation.

A: Are you OK?
B: No, I'm hurt. Where can I get help?
A: The hospital is in the next block.
B: Thank you. Will you go with me?

 Trace the word. Name the letters.

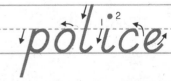

police

 **Draw a line.**

hospital   ambulance   paramedic   victim

nurse   police officer   police car   firefighter

Write the letter. Say the word.

1. __ ictim

2. e __ ergency

3. po __ ice officer

4. __ urse

5. __ uiet

6. phone boo __

 Write your phone number.

_____

- -

_____

  Ask two classmates to write their phone numbers.

_____

- -

1. _____

_____

- -

2. _____

Medical Information

Date __8/31/94__

Name __Wong__ __Albert__
　　　Last Name　　First Name

Address __156 Front Street__
　　　　　　　　Street

__New York__　__NY__　__10038__
　City　　　State　　Zip Code

Date of Birth __3/29/79__　Age __15__

Health ☒ excellent　☐ good　☐ fair

Date of last Medical Examination __7/30/93__

Date of last Dental Checkup __6/14/93__

Date of last Eye Examination __7/30/93__

Immunizations up-to-date ☒ yes　☐ no

Listen to the teacher. Do the actions.

Fill out the form.
Put an **X** in the box.
Give me the form.

Trace the word. Name the letters.

excellent

Months of the Year

1 January 1979	2 February 1979	3 March 1979	4 April 1979
S M T W T F S	S M T W T F S	S M T W T F S	S M T W T F S
1 2 3 4 5 6	1 2 3	1 2 3	1 2 3 4 5 6 7
7 8 9 10 11 12 13	4 5 6 7 8 9 10	4 5 6 7 8 9 10	8 9 10 11 12 13 14
14 15 16 17 18 19 20	11 12 13 14 15 16 17	11 12 13 14 15 16 17	15 16 17 18 19 20 21
21 22 23 24 25 26 27	18 19 20 21 22 23 24	18 19 20 21 22 23 24	22 23 24 25 26 27 28
28 29 30 31	25 26 27 28	25 26 27 28 29 30 31	29 30

5 May 1979	6 June 1979	7 July 1979	8 August 1979
S M T W T F S	S M T W T F S	S M T W T F S	S M T W T F S
1 2 3 4 5	1 2	1 2 3 4 5 6 7	1 2 3 4
6 7 8 9 10 11 12	3 4 5 6 7 8 9	8 9 10 11 12 13 14	5 6 7 8 9 10 11
13 14 15 16 17 18 19	10 11 12 13 14 15 16	15 16 17 18 19 20 21	12 13 14 15 16 17 18
20 21 22 23 24 25 26	17 18 19 20 21 22 23	22 23 24 25 26 27 28	19 20 21 22 23 24 25
27 28 29 30 31	24 25 26 27 28 29 30	29 30 31	26 27 28 29 30 31

9 September 1979	10 October 1979	11 November 1979	12 December 1979
S M T W T F S	S M T W T F S	S M T W T F S	S M T W T F S
1	1 2 3 4 5 6	1 2 3	1
2 3 4 5 6 7 8	7 8 9 10 11 12 13	4 5 6 7 8 9 10	2 3 4 5 6 7 8
9 10 11 12 13 14 15	14 15 16 17 18 19 20	11 12 13 14 15 16 17	9 10 11 12 13 14 15
16 17 18 19 20 21 22	21 22 23 24 25 26 27	18 19 20 21 22 23 24	16 17 18 19 20 21 22
23 24 25 26 27 28 29	28 29 30 31	25 26 27 28 29 30	23 24 25 26 27 28 29
30			30 31

Date of Birth: _____3/29/79_____
                 month   day   year

Say the conversation.

A: Is your name Albert Wong?
B: Yes.
A: What is your date of birth?
B: March 29, 1979.

Trace the word. Name the letters.

January

 **Draw a line.**

1. Date of birth   ☒ excellent   ☐ good   ☐ fair

2. Health   94401

3. Immunizations
   up-to-date   3/29/79

4. Zip Code   555-2241

5. Phone number   ☒ yes   ☐ no

 Listen to the teacher. Circle the month of the year.

1. March ⟨January⟩	2. February July	3. March May
4. August April	5. May July	6. January June
7. June July	8. August October	9. September November
10. October December	11. March November	12. December January

dentist **teeth**   **receptionist**   **Yellow Pages**   **physician** **mouth**

Ching, Steven, DDS   1531 Oak Street   555-5529
Denton, Andrew, DDS   1725 Elm Street   555-2347
Díaz, María, DDS   643 Branch Avenue   555-7421

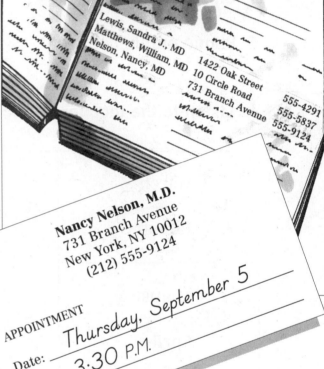

Lewis, Sandra J., MD   1422 Oak Street   555-4291
Matthews, William, MD   10 Circle Road   555-5837
Nelson, Nancy, MD   731 Branch Avenue   555-9124

Nancy Nelson, M.D.
731 Branch Avenue
New York, NY 10012
(212) 555-9124

APPOINTMENT

Date: _Thursday, September 5_

Time: _3:30 P.M._

Listen to the teacher.
Do the actions.

Touch your stomach.
Turn your head.
Breathe in.
Breathe out.

Trace the word. Name the letters.

Yellow Pages

Circle the word.

1.   physician   dentist

2.   appointment   immunization form

3.   Yellow Pages   phone number

4.   physician   receptionist

5.   appointment   medical information

Draw a line.

Andrew Denton, D.D.S.
1725 Elm _____
New York, NY _____
(_____) 555-7421

APPOINTMENT

Date: _____

Time: _____

1. 212

2. 4:15 P.M.

3. Street

4. April 8

5. 10036

waiting room

Insurance Card
Patient: **Albert Wong**
Group Number: **CVW 473241A**
Date of Birth: **3/29/79**

insurance card

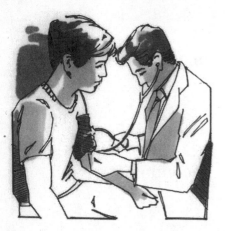

examination room

X ray

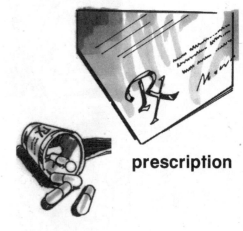

prescription

medicine

 Say the conversation.

A: Albert, you need this medicine.
B: How many days should I take it?
A: Five days. Then you need a follow-up visit.

 Trace the word. Name the letters.

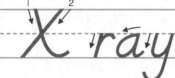

Circle the word.

1. appointment   insurance

2. medical information   Yellow Pages

3. appointment   immunizations

4. medical information   Yellow Pages

Draw a line.

1. medicine

2. examination room

3. waiting room

4. X ray

Write the letter. Say the word.

J j   X x   Y y

1. __ r a y

2. __ a n u a r y

3. e __ c e l l e n t

4. __ e l l o w P a g e s

5. __ e s

6. __ u l y

 Write your date of birth.

_____

- -

_____

  Ask two classmates to write their dates of birth. Write them on the lines.

_____

I. _____

2. _____

Unit 5: Family

Miguel and Yanira's wedding

groom

son

father   mother

bride   **daughter**

parents

 Listen to the teacher. Do the actions.

Look at the camera.
Smile.
Don't move.

 Trace the word. Name the letters.

bride

parents
Yanira
older sister
younger sister
younger brother

Yanira's family

children   younger brothers

mother
father
Miguel

Miguel's family

 Say the conversation.

A: How many children are in Yanira's family?
B: Four. She has an older sister, a younger sister, and a younger brother.
A: How about Miguel?
B: He has three younger brothers.

 Trace the word. Name the letters.

sister

Draw a line.

1. mother

2. younger brother

3. older sister

4. father

5. younger sister

Yanira's family

 Circle the word.

Miguel's family

1.

bride

groom

2.

parents

brothers

3.

parents

children

4.

older brothers

younger brothers

Miguel's Family

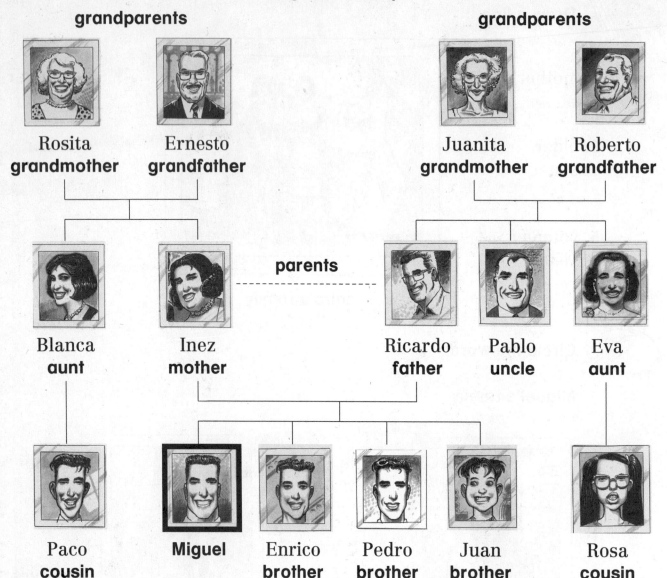

grandparents

Rosita
grandmother

Ernesto
grandfather

grandparents

Juanita
grandmother

Roberto
grandfather

parents

Blanca
aunt

Inez
mother

Ricardo
father

Pablo
uncle

Eva
aunt

Paco
cousin

Miguel

Enrico
brother

Pedro
brother

Juan
brother

Rosa
cousin

Listen to the teacher. Do the actions.

Point to one of Miguel's grandmothers.
Point to Miguel's uncle.
Point to Miguel's cousins.

Trace the word. Name the letters.

grandmother

Circle the word.

Miguel's Family

1. mother   grandmother

2. grandfather   father

3. parents   grandparents

4. father   aunt

 Draw a line.

1. cousin

2. brother

3. parents

4. uncle

5. aunt

Ricardo   Inez

Rosa

Eva

Pablo

Pedro

Yanira's photos

baby

child

teenager

adult

 Say the conversation.

A: Show me your photos.
B: I'm a baby in this photo.
A: Are you a teenager in this photo?
B: Yes, I am.

 Trace the word. Name the letters.

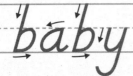

Draw a line.

1. child

2. teenager

3. baby

4. adult

 Write the words in order.

child   adult   teenager   baby

1. _____

2. _____

3. _____

4. _____

Write the letters. Say the words.

1. f __ m i l y

2. s __ s t e r

3. b __ b y

4. b r __ d __

 Who is in your family? Write their names.

1. _____

2. _____

3. _____

4. _____

5. _____

★ ★

Unit 6: Food

Menu

Salads	**Sandwiches/Pizza**	**Side Orders**
green salad	fish sandwich	French fries
chicken salad	hamburger	pickle
fruit salad	sausage/cheese pizza	

Desserts	**Beverages**
ice cream	coffee hot tea
cookies	lemonade iced tea
	soda milk shake

restaurant

Listen to the teacher. Do the actions.

Look at the menu.
Choose your food.
Pay for your food.

Trace the word. Name the letters.

menu

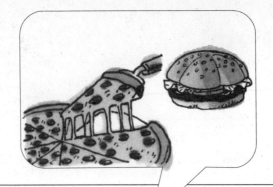

Menu

Salads
green salad
chicken salad
fruit salad

Sandwiches/Pizza
fish sandwich
hamburger
sausage/cheese pizza

Side Orders
French fries
pickle

Desserts
ice cream
cookies

Beverages
coffee   hot tea
lemonade   iced tea
soda   milk shake

 Say the conversation.

A: Are you ready to order?
B: Yes. I'd like a hamburger, French fries, and a milk shake.
A: That's $3.25.
B: Here's $5.00.
A: Thank you. Your change is $1.75.

 Trace the words. Name the letters.

hot tea

Circle the word.

 1. sandwich
pizza

 2. coffee
soda

 3. salad
ice cream

 4. French fries
pickle

 5. sandwich
salad

 Draw a line from the food to the category.

 1.   salads

 2.   desserts

 3.   sandwiches/pizza

 4.   beverages

 5.   side orders

grocery store

 Listen to the teacher. Do the actions.

Push the cart.
Pick up the box.
Look for the vegetables.

 Trace the words. Name the letters.

grocery store

Circle the word.

1.
eggs
cheese

2.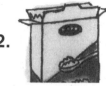
milk
cereal

3.
fruit
vegetables

4.
restaurant
grocery store

5.
fruit
flour

 Draw a line.

1. chicken

2. cheese

3. sugar

4. fruit

5. milk

Money

coins

a penny
1¢
$0.01

a nickel
5¢
$0.05

a dime
10¢
$0.10

a quarter
25¢
$0.25

bills

one dollar
$1.00

five dollars
$5.00

ten dollars
$10.00

twenty
dollars
$20.00

How much is it?

$1.46

$7.33

 Say the conversation.

A: How much are these?
B: They're $2.27.
A: Here's $5.00.
B: Your change is $2.73.

 Trace the word. Name the letters.

Draw a line.

 1. $11.05

 2. $0.68

 3. $0.66

 4. $2.32

 Add. Circle the number.

1.  $1.45 $1.50

2.  $1.42 $1.24

3.  $1.75 $1.90

4.  $2.90 $2.75

Write the letters. Say the word.

1. m __ n u

2. g r __ c e r y   s t o r e

3. m __ __ t

4. s __ d a

5. h __ t   t __ __

6. c h __ __ s e

 Write your favorite food.

_____

- -

_____

 Ask two classmates their favorite foods.
Write their favorite foods on the lines.

- -

1. _____

- -

_____

- -

2. _____

_____

- -

Unit 7: Shopping

mall

clothing store   **shoe store**   **department store**   **music store**   **drugstore**

Listen to the teacher. Do the actions.

Point to the department store.
Point to the clothing store.
Show me the drugstore.

Trace the word. Name the letters.

drugstore

CD   T-shirt   shoes   toothbrush   dress   swimsuit

jeans   socks   CD player   TV   toothpaste   make-up

 Say the conversation.

A: Where can I buy jeans?
B: You can find them at Laura's Jeans.
A: Can I buy T-shirts there too?
B: Yes, you can.

 Trace the word. Name the letters.

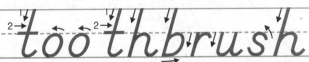
toothbrush

Circle the word.

1.  toothpaste
   toothbrush

2.  TV
   CD

3.   shoes
   socks

4.  swimsuit
   make-up

5.  dress
   T-shirt

 Draw a line.

1. shoe store

2. music store

3. clothing store

4. drugstore

5. department store

Big Sale!

customer   salesperson

price tag

Action Shoes
Big Tree Mall
Atlanta, GA 30320
(404)555-0101

Date _May 11, 1994_

Qty.	Item	Price
1	MJ Tennis Shoes,	$100.00
	Sale 20% off	-20.00
Tax 5%		$80.00
Total		
		4.00
		$84.00

sales slip

cashier

 Listen to the teacher. Do the actions.

Try on the shoes.
Take the sales slip.
Pay the cashier.

 Trace the word. Name the letters.

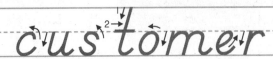

Draw a line.

1. price tag

2. customer

3. sales slip

4. cashier

Circle the price.

1. 　　$120.00　　$180.00

2. 　　$68.00　　$12.00

3. 　　$150.00　　$125.00

4. 　　$32.00　　$40.00

Laura's Jeans
Big Tree Mall
Atlanta, GA 30320
(404) 555-1530

Date _August 20, 1994_

Qty.	Item	Price
1	Jeans, Size 12	$48.00
1	T-Shirt, Size M	14.00
Tax 5%		$62.00
Total		3.10
		$65.10

sales slip

cash

State Bank

2480 0610 27946
Account Number

2/98
Exp. Date

Gloria Martínez
Name

credit card

Gloria Martínez
462 White Birch Street
Atlanta, GA 30317
(404) 555-3051

747

August 20, 19 94

PAY TO THE
ORDER OF _Laura's Jeans_ $ 65.10

Sixty-five and 10/100 —————— DOLLARS

State Bank
Big Tree Mall
Atlanta, GA 30320
(404) 555-1000

Gloria Martínez

MEMO _____

⑆071248003⑆248006 ⑈027946⑈ 0747

check

 Say the conversation.

A: That'll be $65.10.
How do you want to pay?
B: Do you accept checks?
A: Yes, we do.
B: Then I'll give you a check.

Circle the word.

1. credit card   check

2. salesperson   sales slip

3. credit card   cash

4. check   sales slip

5. cashier   credit card

Draw a line.

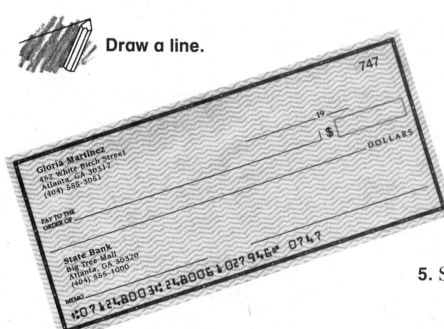

1. *Gloria Martínez*

2. October 12, 1994

3. Sam's Shoes

4. 79.46

5. Seventy-nine and 46/100 —

Write the letters. Say the word.

1. c __ s t o m e r

2. d r __ g s t o r e

3. s w i m s __ __ t

4. t o o t h b r __ s h

5. f r __ __ t

 Write two things you want to buy.

1. _____

2. _____

  Ask two classmates to write something they want to buy.

1. _____

2. _____

Unit 8: Getting Things Done

Getting a Driver's License

To get a **driver's license,** you must

1. be at least 16 years old.

2. take a driving class.

3. study the rules in the driver's manual.

4. take a written test.

5. take an eye test.

6. take a driving test.

Listen to the teacher. Do the actions.

Go.
Stop.
Back up.

Trace the word. Say the word.

Traffic Signs

stop

one way

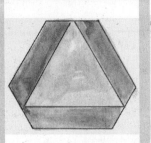
slow

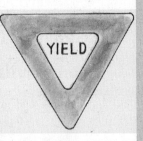
yield

school zone

pedestrian crossing

no left turn

no parking

 Say the conversation.

A: When's your birthday?
B: It's on Wednesday.
A: When are you taking your driving test?
B: On Wednesday, of course!

 Trace the word. Say the word.

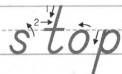
stop

Draw a line.

1.

no left turn

2.

no parking

3.

one way

4.

yield

5.

pedestrian crossing

 Circle the word.

1.
eye test
driving test

2.
traffic signs
school zone

3.
eye test
driving test

4.
driver's manual
driver's license

5.
driving test
driver's manual

Getting a Library Card

librarian

checkout

return

library

application

West Side Public Library
1515 Telegraph Street
Detroit, MI 48239
(313) 555-1167

APPLICATION FOR A LIBRARY CARD   Date 12/16/94

Name _Ramírez,_ _Carlos_
Last Name   First Name

Address _504 Ava Street_   Apt. _16_
Street

Detroit   _MI_   _48234_
City   State   ZIP

Phone number _(313) 555-7986_

Name of Parent _Lidia Ramírez_
(If under 18 years old)

I will be responsible for the materials I check out.

Signature _Carlos Ramírez_

Lidia Ramírez

Signature of Parent
(If under 18 years old)

identification

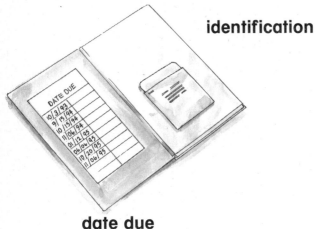

date due

DEC DETROIT AREA ELECTRIC COMPANY
10675 MICHIGAN AVENUE
DETROIT, MI 48210

PRESORTED
FIRST-CLASS MAIL
U.S. POSTAGE PAID
DETROIT, MICHIGAN
PERMIT NO. 27081

Lidia Ramírez
504 Ava Street, Apt. 16
Detroit, MI 48234

library card

7 01678 800413 2705

West Side Public Library
1515 Telegraph Street, Detroit, MI 48239
(313) 555-1167

Print
Name _Carlos Ramírez_

Expiration Date MAY 1998

Listen to the teacher. Do the actions.

Check out the books.
Return the books.
Be quiet.

Trace the word. Say the word.

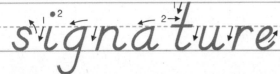

signature

Circle the word.

1. application   date due

2. library card   identification

3. application   library card

4. identification   library card

5. _Carlos Ramírez_   signature   return

 Draw a line.

1. librarian

2. checkout

3. return

4. library card

Going to the Post Office

post office

letter

stamp

envelope

package

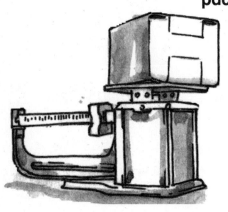

package notice

 Say the conversation.

A: What can I do for you?
B: I want to send this package.
A: That's $3.25.
B: Here you are. I also need some stamps.

 Trace the word. Say the word.

package

Draw a line.

1. package

2. package notice

3. stamps

4. envelope

 Circle the word.

1.    letter   envelope

2.    package   stamps

3. 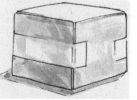   letter   envelope

4.   package   package notice

5.    library   post office

Write the letter. Say the word.

1. p __ c k a g e   2. __ n v e l o p e

3. n o t __ c e   4. s t __ p

5. t __ s t   6. t r __ f f i c

 Send this letter to your school. Address the envelope.

 Complete the postal form.

**Authorization
to Hold Mail**

UNITED STATES
POSTAL SERVICE

Postmaster - Please hold mail for: _____

Name(s)

_____

Address

Begin Holding Mail (Date)	Resume Delivery (Date)

Unit 9: Jobs

child-care worker

I need a job.

What kind of job do you want?

restaurant worker

receptionist

driver

waitress

salesperson

data-entry clerk

checkout person

Listen to the teacher. Do the actions.

Make a phone call.
Clear the table.
Drive the truck.

Trace the words. Say the words.

child care

How do I find a job?

Look in these places.

career center

job announcements

JOB BOARD

counselor

JOBS

INDEX

classified ads

manager

sign

HELP WANTED INQUIRE WITHIN

RESUME
ANA GUADALUPE LOPEZ
772 MOUNTAIN WAY
TOLEDO, OH 42603
(419) 555-9745

WORK EXPERIENCE

EDUCATION

OTHER QUALIFICAT

resume

 Say the conversation.

A: Excuse me. I'm looking for a job.
B: Come in. What kind of qualifications do you have?
A: Here is my resume. I have experience working as a checkout person.
B: Good. Here's an application. Fill it out, please.

HELP WANTED INQUIRE WITHIN

 Trace the word. Say the word.

qualifications

‹‹

Circle the word.

 1.
receptionist

data-entry clerk

 3.
driver

checkout person

 5.
receptionist

restaurant worker

2.
child-care worker

waitress

4.
salesperson

waitress

 Draw a line.

 1.

classified ads

 2.

counselor

 3.

resume

 4.

career center

 5.

sign

part-time job

full-time job

temporary job

permanent job

salary

benefits

 Listen to the teacher. Do the actions.

Introduce yourself.
Shake hands.
Sit down.

 Trace the words. Say the words.

part-time job

Draw a line.

1.
Manager
Suburban store seeks reliable manager for night shifts. Experience in retail sales necessary. Salary mid to upper 20s. **Good Insurance.** Send resume to Box M21, Chicago, IL 60622.

2.
Bank Teller
Riverton Bank is now hiring for temporary positiions at our Main Street location. **6/15 — 8/15,** 40 hrs/wk. Call Janet Battiste at (312)555-2848.

3.
Data-Entry Clerk
If you're an experienced data-entry clerk, you can earn **$9.00/hr**, approximately 20 hours per week with our growing company.

4.
Child-Care Worker
3 children. Mon.-Fri. **9 A.M. - 5 P.M.** Bilingual speaker preferred. Experience and references required. Naperville area. Call after 5 P.M. (708) 555-2046.

5.
Restaurant
Chomps Bar and Grill now hiring waitstaff and kitchen workers. Hours available from **4 P.M.-8 P.M.** weekdays. Apply in person between 2-4 P.M.

full-time job

benefits

salary

part-time job

temporary job

Circle the job.

I want to work on Saturdays.

full-time job

part-time job

I like children.

child-care worker

receptionist

I need to work eight hours every day.

full-time job

part-time job

I have a driver's license.

waitress

driver

I want a job for one month.

permanent job

temporary job

How do I get training?

Here are some places to get training.

high school

secretary

community college

medical technician

vocational school

mechanic

on-the-job training

bank teller

 Say the conversation.

A: I want to be a medical technician.
B: You can take classes in the afternoon at the community college.
A: I also want to take English classes.
B: Good. You can take English classes in the morning at the high school.

 Trace the words. Say the words.

community college

Draw a line.

mechanic

receptionist

bank teller

medical technician

 Circle the word.

1.
high school

community college

2.
high school

on-the-job training

3.
vocational school

community college

4.
high school

vocational school

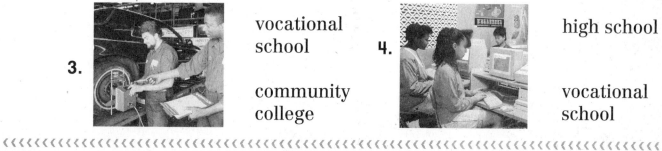

Write the letter. Say the word.

1. s __ l e s p e r s o n

2. e x p __ r i e n c e

3. d r __ v e r

4. g r __ c e r y

5. r e s __ m e

6. c h __ l d   c a r e

7. c o m m __ n i t y

8. w __ __ t r e s s

 Write the words for two jobs you want.

1. _____

2. _____

  Ask two classmates to write the words for jobs they want.

1. _____

2. _____